Introduction

One of the most important players on any baseball team is the catcher. He is the man who tells the pitcher what pitch to throw. A catcher has to study the batters so that he can signal for pitches which will fool them. He also needs a strong arm so that he can pick runners off base and throw them out stealing. Team managers like their catchers to be powerful hitters, too.

This is the story of one of the greatest catchers in the game: Johnny Bench of the Cincinnati Reds.

Sports Hero

Johnny Bench

by Marshall and Sue Burchard

G. P. Putnam's Sons • New York

We wish to thank Mr. Doyle Marlett for his kind help.

PHOTO CREDITS

Mr. Doyle Marlett, pp. 9, 13, 14, 22, 24, 95.
United Press International, pp. 2, 38, 41, 46, 49, 54, 56, 61, 63, 64, 67, 68, 71, 72, 76, 81, 84, 90, 93.

Illustrations by Paul Frame

27403

Sixth Impression

SBN: GB-399-60739-0
SBN: TR-399-20246-3
Library of Congress Catalog Card Number: 79-179378
PRINTED IN THE UNITED STATES OF AMERICA

Contents

1

Growing Up in
Oklahoma

Johnny Bench was born on December 7, 1947, in Oklahoma City, Oklahoma. While he was a little boy, his family lived in nearby Lindsay, Oklahoma. As far back as Johnny can remember, he played baseball. When he was three years old, he played catch in the backyard with his father. Sometimes his older brothers, William and Teddy, played, too.

When Johnny was four years old, he watched a baseball game on TV. He heard the announcer talk about a player from Oklahoma named Mickey Mantle. The announcer said that Mantle was going to be a big star. Little Johnny Bench began dreaming. At four years old, he made up his mind. He was going to be a professional baseball player just like Mickey Mantle.

The following year his family

Downtown Binger.

moved to Binger, Oklahoma. Binger is a very small town. There are only 650 people living there. There are only two blocks of stores. Most of the people who live in Binger are farmers. They grow some cotton. But mainly, they grow peanuts.

Ted Bench, Johnny's father, had several jobs in Binger to earn money for his family. For a while he sold furniture. He also sold natural gas. He delivered the gas in a truck to people who lived in Binger.

Johnny's father would much rather have earned a living playing baseball. He was a promising young catcher before he was called into the Army in World War II. While he was fighting in North Africa, he was wounded in the arm. That ended his hope of becoming a major-league catcher.

Ted Bench spent as much time as he could teaching his three sons to play baseball. If he couldn't be a big-league catcher himself, maybe one of his boys could. William was five years older than Johnny. Teddy was six years older. They were willing to play with their younger brother, but they would never let him win. Johnny had to play hard to keep up with them.

Binger was such a small town

that it didn't have a Little League team. Johnny's father tried to start one so that his boys could play on a team. It was hard to get enough players to come out for the games. Finally, Mr. Bench gave up.

One day he piled his three sons in the back of his truck and drove twenty miles to Fort Cobb, Oklahoma. For two years he drove his sons back and forth from Fort Cobb to play on the Little League team there.

When he was able to round up enough players, Mr. Bench got

Binger Little League field.

the Binger Little League team going again. It thrilled him to see his youngest son play. He had a feeling that someday Johnny would make baseball history.

Binger High School.

2

High School Star

Johnny Bench was one of the greatest athletes who ever went to Binger High School. He played whatever sport was in season. He was good at everything. He won all-state honors in baseball and basketball. He probably would have won all-state honors in football, too, but Binger High didn't have a football team.

Johnny played guard on the Binger basketball team. He had an advantage over the other players. He had such big hands that he could grip a basketball in one hand. (Later he was able to hold seven baseballs in one hand!) His enormous hands made him a very good ball handler. He averaged 23 points, 17 rebounds, and 13 assists a game.

By the time he was a senior in high school he was six feet one inch tall. Many of the other basketball players were taller. But Johnny learned to jump higher than they did. He learned to jump so high that he could "dunk" the ball by stuffing it down through the basket.

Good as he was at basketball, Johnny was even better at baseball. He could throw the ball straight and hard. He became a pitcher for Binger High. He pitched 16 games and won all but one of them. The score of the game he lost was 2 to 0, and the two runs scored were not his fault. They were the result of fielding errors. He pitched several no-hit games.

An accident almost ended Johnny's promising career. He was riding with the rest of the baseball team on the school bus one day on the way to a game. The brakes on the bus failed. The bus went out of control and rammed into a guardrail. It plunged down a steep embankment. Two members of the team were killed. Johnny was thrown down the aisle of the bus and up against the back door.

The door was jarred open. Johnny was found with his leg sticking out the door. He only had a few bruises, but he was badly frightened.

The high school team did not play baseball often enough to satisfy Johnny. So when he was fifteen, he started playing for an American Legion team in nearby Anadarko, Oklahoma. Anadarko is two miles south of Binger. Johnny wanted to play catcher. but the team already had two catchers several years older than

Johnny. So he pitched or played first or third base.

When Johnny was a senior in high school, the manager of the American Legion team decided to play him at first base all the time. Johnny's father thought that was a mistake. He knew that scouts from several major-league teams already had their eye on Johnny. He was sure his son would make a better showing as a catcher. Mr. Bench had not interfered with Johnny's career for a long time. But now he felt it was time to step in. He went to see the manager of the team.

"Catch Johnny or he doesn't play," said Mr. Bench. The manager made Johnny the catcher.

In his spare time Johnny did

The house Johnny grew up in.

many odd jobs to earn money. He chopped cotton. He mowed lawns. He delivered newspapers. When he was sixteen, he drove a tank truck full of liquefied petroleum. Whatever job Johnny had, Ted Bench made sure his son never missed a baseball game. Baseball always came first.

In class Johnny was an enthusiastic student. He made straight A's. He did so well that he was made valedictorian of his high school class. On graduation day he made a speech to students and parents. He said people from his generation would be tomorrow's leaders. For him, the prediction came true.

3

Turning Pro

Seventeen colleges offered Johnny scholarships if he would come play basketball. But he wasn't interested. He was determined to play baseball.

After being graduated from high school, he played catcher for an American Legion baseball team in Oklahoma City. Scouts from the major-league teams came to watch him play.

In late June two scouts from the Cincinnati Reds showed up at the baseball field to watch a couple of games. They saw Johnny go to bat eight times. He made only one hit. But still, the Cincinnati scouts asked him to come play for their team. They liked the way he threw the ball. They also liked the way he moved around behind the plate. They were sure he would make a fine catcher.

Usually new baseball players do not play for a major-league club right away. A new player starts out playing for minor-league teams and works his way up to the major leagues. Cincinnati sent Johnny to play for their minor-league team in Tampa, Florida. The team was called the Tampa Tarpons. They played in the Florida Instructional League.

Johnny didn't waste any time. His train arrived in Tampa at 8:57 P.M. He immediately rushed to the ball park. He got there just in time to be the catcher for the ninth inning of the Tarpons' game that night.

The next day he took over as the Tarpons' regular catcher.

The Tampa manager had Johnny hit next to last in the batting order. The manager knew that Johnny could become a powerful hitter someday. But first he would have to get used to batting against professional pitchers.

The Tampa manager was named Dave Bristol. Bristol sat down with his young catcher before each game and went over scouting reports on the team the Tarpons were playing against.

The reports told Johnny what kinds of batters the other team had and what pitches to signal for in order to get them out. Johnny was smart. He remembered to use what he learned about the opposing batters when they came to the plate in the game.

Dave Bristol was pleased with his seventeen-year-old catcher.

"Bench is my kind of guy," he said. "He wants to win, and he wants to learn. Besides that, he's got tremendous ability. He has a great arm and good power. He sets up hitters like an old hand."

4

Trouble on the Way Up

The next spring the Cincinnati Reds gave Johnny a promotion. They sent him to Hampton, Virginia, to play for the Peninsula team in the Carolina League.

Johnny got off to a slow start at bat. But once he got used to the pitchers, there was no stopping him. The manager moved him into the fourth position in the batting order. Hitting "clean-up" suited Johnny just fine. In 98 games for Peninsula he hit 22 home runs. That was a club record.

Midway through the season the Cincinnati Reds decided it was time to promote Johnny again. They sent word for him to report immediately to Buffalo, New York, to play for the Buffalo Bisons in the International League.

The Peninsula team didn't

want to let Johnny go off without honoring him for having been such a fine player. So they made a rule that no Peninsula player could ever again wear Number 19, the number Johnny had worn on his uniform. The night he left for Buffalo, his fans came to say good-bye. They escorted him out of town at the head of a parade. Nobody seemed to notice that it was raining.

Johnny arrived in Buffalo on July 31 and went straight to the ball park for a game. Almost at once he had an unfortunate accident. In the first inning he tried to catch a foul tip with his bare right hand. The ball hit his thumb and broke the bone.

The broken bone would take weeks to heal. Johnny was through playing baseball for the rest of the season. He was very disappointed. There was nothing he could do but go back home to Binger and wait for the next season to roll around.

Before it did, another accident almost finished Johnny's career forever. He was driving his car one day when another car came toward him going the wrong way on a freeway exit. He tried to swerve, but it was too late. The cars collided head on.

In one way Johnny was lucky. There was a doctor in the car behind him. The doctor stopped and gave Johnny first aid. Some-one called for an ambulance.

It seemed like a very long ride to the hospital. Johnny could not tell how badly he was hurt. His head and shoulder were bleeding. It was painful for him to twist his

body. He was afraid he might end up being a cripple and never play baseball again.

At the hospital doctors took sixteen stitches in his head and fourteen in his shoulder. The doctors said the rest of his body was only bruised. They told him that if he weren't big-boned and strong, he would have surely had a broken hip.

5

Breaking into the
Big Leagues

By the start of the 1967
baseball season Johnny was
healthy again and back in the
Buffalo lineup as catcher. For the
first two months of the season he
didn't get very many hits. It took
him awhile to get used to the
International League pitchers.
He was also a little out of
practice. He had missed most of

spring training because he had to be away at an Army reserve camp.

Dave Bristol wasn't worried. He said, "Johnny will need a little time, but he'll adjust." Bristol knew what he was talking about. Johnny eventually started hitting, and by August he had a fine batting average. He had socked 23 homers and driven in more runs than any other player in the league.

The Cincinnati Reds felt their promising young catcher was ready for the big leagues. On

Manager Bristol welcomes Johnny to the Reds.

August 25, 1967, Johnny Bench went to play for the Reds.

Dave Bristol had just become the Reds' manager. He made Johnny his number one catcher right away. At first, Johnny was a little embarrassed. He was only nineteen years old. There were three good catchers on the team already. He wasn't sure he deserved to play ahead of them yet. He didn't want to disappoint the team and his fans.

Throughout the National League, players had heard stories about what a great throwing arm

Johnny had. They wondered if he could really throw the ball as hard and straight as people said he could.

They soon found out. In less than a week Johnny picked off his first player at first base. He was able to get rid of the ball with amazing quickness. It became almost impossible for anyone to steal a base when he was catching.

Even the fastest base runners had trouble beating him. Lou Brock of the St. Louis Cardinals hadn't been thrown out stealing all season, until he came up against Johnny. Brock had stolen 21 bases in a row. But when he tried for number 22, Johnny threw him out at second base.

At first Johnny had trouble hitting major-league pitching. In his first 88 trips to the plate, he made only 14 hits. But during September he got hot. In one game against the Atlanta Braves in Atlanta, he pounded out 3 hits. One of them was his first major-league home run. He hit 4 more homers that month.

Three days before the end of

the season he was put out of action again. The Reds were playing the Cubs at Wrigley Field in Chicago. One of the Chicago batters fouled off a pitch, and again Johnny's thumb got in the way. Fortunately this time the bone wasn't broken. But the thumb was badly cut, and Johnny had to sit out the last two games.

It was still a great year for Johnny. He was elected Minor League Player of the Year for his play at Buffalo. More awards were soon to follow.

The confident rookie.

6

Rookie of the Year

Johnny returned to the Reds' training camp in 1968 feeling very good. He was looking forward to his first full season in the major leagues. He was even a little cocky about his ability. He told reporters that he was going to win the Rookie of the Year Award.

Ted Williams, the great Boston Red Sox slugger, came to watch Cincinnati in training. He was very impressed with the way Johnny played. It was a big moment for Johnny to meet Ted Williams. Ted had been a boyhood hero. After practice, Johnny asked for Ted's autograph on a baseball. Ted wrote, "To Johnny, a Hall of Famer for sure." The ball is one of Johnny's most prized possessions.

When the season started, Johnny continued to strike fear into the hearts of enemy base

Picking off a runner at second base.

runners with his deadly throws. The reason he can throw so well is that his arm is very big and strong. It is about as big around as a normal man's leg. Most pitchers don't have as strong a throwing arm as Johnny.

He gave a remarkable demonstration of his throwing power one day in the sixth inning of a game against the Los Angeles Dodgers. Ron Fairly was the first Dodger batter. He hit a double. Moments later he tried to steal third base. Johnny threw him out. Tom Haller came to bat and walked. On a wild pitch he tried for second base. Johnny recovered the ball and fired off his throw in time to catch Haller for the second out. The next Dodger batter made what seemed to be a perfect bunt. But Johnny fielded the ball swiftly and threw the runner out at first base. Three up and three down, all thanks to the heroic arm of Johnny Bench.

By the end of the season Johnny was becoming well known for his batting as well. He was hitting clean-up, which is something few major-league rookies ever get to do. He had a good batting average. He socked 15 homers and 40 doubles and drove in 82 runs.

At the end of the year he won

the Golden Glove Award as the best defensive catcher in the National League. He played in 154 games, something no rookie catcher had ever done before. To top it off, he was the first catcher in major-league history to be named Rookie of the Year. He won the award by one vote. The runner-up was Jerry Koosman, the twenty-two-year-old left-handed pitcher of the New York Mets.

After all those honors, Johnny had a right to feel a little cocky. He was twenty-one years old, and he was already a big-league star. He was enjoying life. He had a nice apartment in Cincinnati in a building where a lot of young single people lived. He liked going out with pretty girls. He liked going to discothèques and doing dances like the Funky Broadway, the Tighten Up, and Four Corner, and the Horse.

He liked to sing, too. He even thought about having a singing career someday. But for the moment he was doing just fine playing baseball.

Slugging a homer.

7

The Big Red Machine

Johnny Bench and the whole Cincinnati Reds team returned to spring training in 1969 in good spirits. They had high hopes of winning the pennant that year.

Their hopes were pinned on their good hitters. In the early part of the season their chances looked good. There were only twelve players in the entire major leagues that spring who had batting averages of over .300, and six of them played for the Cincinnati Reds. The Reds were such a powerful hitting team that

The Big Red Machine. Surrounding Johnny i
the driver's seat are, left to right, Bobby Tolan
Tony Perez, Lee May and Pete Rose.

people started calling them the Big Red Machine.

Johnny worked hard at his batting. The effort paid off. In one of the Reds' early games he pounded out a single and two doubles, and drove home five runs as Cincinnati walloped Houston by a score of 14 to 0 in the Astrodome.

Getting off to a good start in hitting was new to Johnny. He thought it was because this was the first time he had been in the same league for two years in a row. It helps a batter to know a lot about the pitchers he has to face.

After the first fourteen games, Johnny was leading the league with 16 runs batted in. It was no wonder. The players who batted ahead of him were all fine hitters. Right fielder Pete Rose was batting .360, center fielder Bobby Tolan was batting .333, and third baseman Tony Perez was batting .370. By the time Johnny came to bat there almost had to be somebody on base.

Johnny did so well that he was chosen to be the starting catcher for the National League All-Star team. Playing in the All-Star Game that year meant a great deal to him, but he almost missed his chance. The game was supposed to be played in the middle of the season in Washington, D.C.'s new Robert F. Kennedy Stadium. The problem was that at that time Johnny was off spending two weeks at Army reserve camp. His job at camp was cook's helper. He had to peel potatoes, chop onions, and do other things to get meals ready for several hundred soldiers. After each meal, there were hundreds of dishes to wash.

Johnny certainly didn't want to miss the All-Star Game just because he was supposed to be peeling a few potatoes and washing some dishes. So he talked his commanding officer into giving him a special leave for the day. He rushed to Washington and arrived just in time for the game.

He hit one home run and came within inches of hitting another. The National League won by a score of 8 to 2. After the game

Vice President Agnew throws out the first ball to start the 1969 All-Star game.

Johnny shook hands with President Nixon and chatted with Vice President Agnew. Then he rushed back to Army camp to face a mountain of dirty pots and pans.

When his hitch at Army camp was finished, Johnny returned to the Cincinnati lineup. He had a good year. He finished the season with a batting average of .293. He had 26 homers and 90 runs batted in.

The only trouble was that the Big Red Machine did not win the pennant. They scored more runs than any other team in the major leagues that year, but their pitchers gave up a lot of runs, too. In the end the Reds came in third in their division.

Johnny slides home safely with a run.

Manager Sparky Anderson.

8

Winning the Pennant

Before the 1970 season began, the Cincinnati Reds got a new manager. His name was Sparky Anderson. He was only thirty-six years old. He was the youngest manager in the major leagues. Before coming to the Reds, he had spent five years managing minor-league teams. All his teams had been winners.

The Reds rallied around their new manager. They got off to such a good start that soon all Cincinnati was talking about the team's chances of capturing the pennant. When the Reds won their games, which was most of the time, their fans would shout, "The Big Red Machine won again! Let's hear it for the Machine! Yea, Machine!" All over town drivers proudly plastered their car bumpers with stickers that said BIG RED MACHINE.

Johnny Bench, Tony Perez,

and the other Reds' sluggers were knocking out home runs faster than ever. But the big difference was that the Cincinnati pitching had improved. In Jim Merritt, Jim McGlothlin, Wayne Simp-

familiar sight: Johnny driving in teammates with a home run.

Jim Merritt.

son, and Gary Nolan, the Reds had four fine young pitchers. They made it hard for the other teams to score many runs.

The Cincinnati pitchers would not have done so well if it had not been for Johnny's alert work behind the plate. He had played in the National League long enough to know the hitters well. He was good at calling for pitches that fooled them. He was also good at scooping up wild pitches thrown in the dirt in front of him. To prevent the low pitches from taking bad bounces, he carefully filled in the holes left in the ground around home plate by each batter's spikes.

Another important way he helped his pitchers was by scaring base runners with his great throwing arm. With Johnny catching, the Cincinnati pitchers didn't have to worry much about anybody stealing a base. Instead of tiring themselves out making pick-off throws, they could forget the base runners and concentrate on pitching to the hitters. If a runner took too big a lead off first base, the pitchers could count on Johnny to pick him off base. And if a runner tried to steal, they knew Johnny would usually cut him down.

By July 1 the Reds were leading the Western Division of the

Johnny tags out Willie Mays.

National League by nine and one-
half games. Soon afterward they
moved from Crosley Field to a

new home ball park called Riverfront Stadium. Their new park was
located beside the Ohio River,
and it was much bigger than their
old one. Some fans were worried
that it was too big. They were
afraid that the Reds would not

New Riverfront Stadium with lights on for a
night game.

be able to hit as many home runs there.

The fans didn't have to worry long. In their first game in the new stadium the Reds smacked three home runs. They beat Montreal by a score of 5 to 1. More than 50,000 people were there to cheer them on. It was the biggest crowd that had ever seen a sports contest in Cincinnati.

By the beginning of August Johnny had slammed out 36 home runs. There were still two months left in the season, and even Johnny was amazed at how well he was hitting.

"I'd be lying if I said I wasn't," he told reporters. "You know how many homers I predicted I'd hit when the season began? Thirty." By the time the season was over he had hit 45 homers, the most anybody in the major leagues hit that year. He also led the major leagues in runs batted in with 148.

The Reds won the race for the Western Division championship easily. Then they beat the Eastern Division champions, the Pittsburgh Pirates, in a three-game play-off for the National League pennant.

Johnny was thrilled. Every ballplayer dreams about playing in the World Series, but not many ever get the chance. Now, after only three years in the major leagues, Johnny was about to live that dream. It was almost too good to be true.

Before the World Series Johnny rubs a statue of Buddha for good luck.

9

World Series

In October the Cincinnati Reds met the Baltimore Orioles in the World Series. The first team to win four games would win the Series and get to fly the World Champion flag at their ball park for a whole year. More important to the players was the fact that each member of the winning team would earn an extra $15,000.

The Baltimore Orioles were an excellent team. They had won the American League pennant just as easily as the Reds had won the National League pennant. The Orioles had a great infield led by third baseman Brooks Robinson, a magician with the glove. They also had strong pitching. Three of the Oriole starters—Mike Cuellar, Dave McNally and Jim Palmer—had each won 20 or more games during the regular season. The Cincinnati pitchers were good, too, but toward the end of the season they had begun being bothered by sore arms.

If Baltimore had the edge in pitching, Cincinnati certainly had the edge in hitting. Johnny Bench was the Reds' top slugger, and Tony Perez was not far behind. Over the season Perez hit 40 homers and batted in 129 runs. Shortstop Bernie Carbo, center fielder Bob Tolan, right fielder Pete Rose, and third baseman Perez all hit over .300 for the year.

A lot of people thought that the Big Red Machine was too strong for the Orioles. They thought the Cincinnati hitters would overpower the Baltimore pitchers.

The Series opened in Cincinnati. The Big Red Machine went to work in the first inning. Bob Tolan doubled. Johnny Bench drove him in with a line-drive single to left field for the first run of the game. The Reds went ahead, 3 to 0, two innings later, when their first baseman, Lee May, hit a homer over the left-field fence with one man on base.

Then all of a sudden the Machine sputtered to a halt. The

Reds' starting pitcher, Gary Nolan, began to tire. In the fourth
inning the Baltimore first baseman, Boog Powell, hit a two-
run homer to make the score
Reds 3, Orioles 2. An inning
later the Baltimore catcher,
Elrod Hendricks, hit a home run
to tie the game at 3 to 3. In the

Baltimore's
Boog Powell
beats Johnny's
tag.

seventh inning the Baltimore third baseman, Brooks Robinson, hit a home run to win the game for the Orioles by a score of 4 to 3.

In the second game in Cincinnati the Reds took an early lead of 4 to 0. But once again the machine ran out of gas. Baltimore caught up. Despite a home run by Johnny Bench in the seventh inning, the Orioles won the game by a score of 6 to 5. Trailing two games to nothing, the Reds headed for Baltimore for the third game of the Series.

In the third game, it looked as if the Reds were going to get something started in the first inning once again. Pete Rose led off with a single, and Bob Tolan beat out a bunt. Then Tony Perez hit into a double play. With two out and a runner on second base, Johnny Bench hit a hard line drive down the third-base line. Brooks Robinson robbed Johnny of a hit with a diving catch to end the inning.

In the sixth inning Johnny came up to bat again. He hit another scorching line drive in the direction of Robinson, and once again the Oriole third baseman robbed him of a hit with an amazing acrobatic catch.

When Robinson came up to

Brooks Robinson snares Johnny's line drive.

bat a little while later, Johnny promised him: "I'm gonna hit the next one over your head."

"Okay," said the always agreeable Oriole star, laughing.

It was not a good day for Cincinnati. The Oriole pitcher, Dave McNally, hit a home run with the bases loaded. Baltimore won easily by a score of 9 to 3. The win put Baltimore ahead three games to none. If Cincinnati lost another game, the Series would be over.

After the game a TV cam-

eraman came into the Cincinnati locker room. The players
were in no mood for picture
taking. Johnny took off his shirt
and hung it over the lens of the
TV camera. The cameraman was
three inches taller than Johnny,
but he didn't complain very hard
about the shirt.

"I'm only trying to do my job,"
the cameraman said.

"Yeah, I know," Bench re-
plied, keeping his shirt draped
over the lens. "Why don't you go
over to the Baltimore locker
room and take your pictures?

You'll get a lot more happy faces over there."

The Cincinnati manager, Sparky Anderson, tried to offer some words of hope to his discouraged players.

"Something's gotta change," he told them. "Things have happened so far that nobody would believe. Everything they do turns out right, and everything we do turns out wrong. I just don't believe it can keep going on that way.

"One thing I feel now," he insisted. "If we beat 'em tomorrow, I feel we'll go all the way."

The Reds did beat the Orioles the next day by a score of 6 to 5. But despite Sparky Anderson's feeling, they were unable to go all the way. In the fifth game of the Series, the Baltimore batters were red hot. The Reds used six pitchers trying to stop them. It was no use. Baltimore made 15 hits to only 6 for Cincinnati and won the game by a score of 9 to 3.

The Orioles were World Champions for 1970. But the Reds had a strong young team. With any luck they might soon win another pennant and get another crack at the World Series. Then things might turn out differently.

Meanwhile, the Cincinnati players could console themselves with the fact that they had each earned an extra $7,500, the loser's share for playing in the Series.

Three stars and their trophies: Johnny Bench "Player of the Year," Brooks Robinson "Defensive Player of the Year," and Bob Gibson "Pitcher of the Year."

10

Most Valuable Player

After the World Series, Johnny collected just about every award in sight. He was named Player of the Year by the newspaper *Sporting News*. The Baseball Writers Association of America awarded him the National League's Most Valuable Player prize. At the age of twenty-three he was the youngest player ever to receive the award.

"This is the greatest," he said when he heard he had won the most Valuable Player honor. "This is what every player dreams of some day. Wow! It's really something."

Johnny found plenty of things to do in the off season. He played in his first Hollywood acting role. He played an Army officer in a *Mission Impossible* TV episode. When it was time for him to appear before the cameras, he was a little nervous. He stepped out on the wrong foot, and the scene had to be filmed again.

Officer Johnny in *Mission Impossible*.

Johnny had an explanation. "When you're a catcher, you just squat down and don't worry about which foot goes first," he said.

In addition to acting, he played

in golf tournaments, made TV commercials and sang in night-clubs. In his spare time, he traveled around the country making appearances for the Reds.

The people of Binger, Oklahoma, were proud of Johnny. They decided to hold a Johnny Bench Day in his honor. Johnny and his father Ted rode up the main street of town together in the back seat of a convertible. They smiled and waved at all the people they passed. The sun shone brightly. The band played loudly. It was a happy day.

hnny and Ted Bench parading through Binger.

The Authors

Marshall and Sue Burchard are married and the parents of two children, Marshall and Wendy. They live in New York City but have spent the past few summers in Spain. Marshall, a former education editor of *Time* magazine is presently a free-lance writer. Sue is a librarian at Trinity School. They have previously written *Sports Hero* biographies of Joe Namath, Brooks Robinson, and Kareem Abdul Jabbar for Putnam.